What Makes Someone a Jew?

Lauren Seidman

JEWISH LIGHTS Publishing

Woodstock, Vermont

What Makes Someone a Jew?

2007 First Printing
Text © 2007 by Lauren Seidman

The author would like to thank Shirley R. Gindler-Price of the Jewish Multiracial Network, Edmund Case and Heather Martin of InterfaithFamily.com, Harriet Bograd of Kulanu, and Karen Gouchberg and Peggy Kasden of Congregation Shir Shalom in Woodstock, Vermont, for their help in obtaining photos. Special thanks to all of the people who submitted photos for this book—I couldn't have done it without you!

Photo credits: page 8 courtesy Claudia Ginanni; page 10 courtesy Amy Shore; pages 12–13, 31 and bottom/middle page 32 courtesy Ruti Rubenstein, professional Israeli photographer (www.specialeyes.co.il; ruti@specialeyes.co.il; 972 52 3939632); page 21 courtesy Bob Johnson; page 22 courtesy Stacey B. Peyer; page 25 courtesy Shellye Horowitz, MA; page 30 courtesy John Liquori (left) and E-vent Images (right).

Library of Congress Cataloging-in-Publication Data

Seidman, Lauren, 1976–
What makes someone a Jew? / Lauren Seidman.
p. cm.
ISBN-13: 978-1-58023-321-7 (pbk.)
ISBN-10: 1-58023-321-X
1. Jewish way of life—Juvenile literature. 2. Jews—Identity—Juvenile literature. 3. Jewish ethics—Juvenile literature. I. Title.
BM723.S379 2007
296—dc22

2006033093

10 9 8 7 6 5 4 3 2 1

Manufactured in Singapore
Cover & interior design: Jenny Buono

Published by Jewish Lights Publishing
A Division of LongHill Partners, Inc.
Sunset Farm Offices, Route 4, P.O. Box 237
Woodstock, VT 05091
Tel: (802) 457-4000   Fax: (802) 457-4004
www.jewishlights.com

What makes a person a Jew?

Is it the way that they look or the things that they do?

You don't have to look
a certain way to be Jewish,
Your eyes can be light, dark,
brownish or bluish.

Skin white, **black**, or golden,
and all colors in between,
You can still be Jewish
if your skin is green!

Your hair can be **black**,

blonde,

brown or

red—

What matters is inside your heart

and inside your head.

Do Jews only come
from one place
on Earth?

Are Jewish people Jewish
from the time of their birth?

It's not where you're born that makes you a Jew,
you can be from Chihuahua,

Giggleswick

or

Timbuktu.

The Jewish People have wandered from land to land,
in cities, up mountains, through hot desert sand.

Some people are born Jewish,
but you don't have to be:
Judaism starts when
you live Jewishly.

Which means being kind
  to the people around you,
Studying the Torah,
  and learning some Hebrew.

א ה י
ל ח ד ב
ק צ ו ע ו
מ ת ש
פ נ ג ט

What else can I do to live Jewishly?

Are there ways to be Jewish with my family?

You can celebrate Hanukkah,
the festival of lights,
Lighting your menorah
on all eight nights.

On **Pesach** have a Seder,
       read the Haggadah,
And look for the afikomen—
       the special hidden matzah!

Go to synagogue on Rosh Hashanah,
       hear the shofar **BLAST**,
The start of a new year,
       the end of one just passed.

And Shabbat comes every weekend,
beginning Friday night,
With challah, fun, and family,
songs and candlelight.

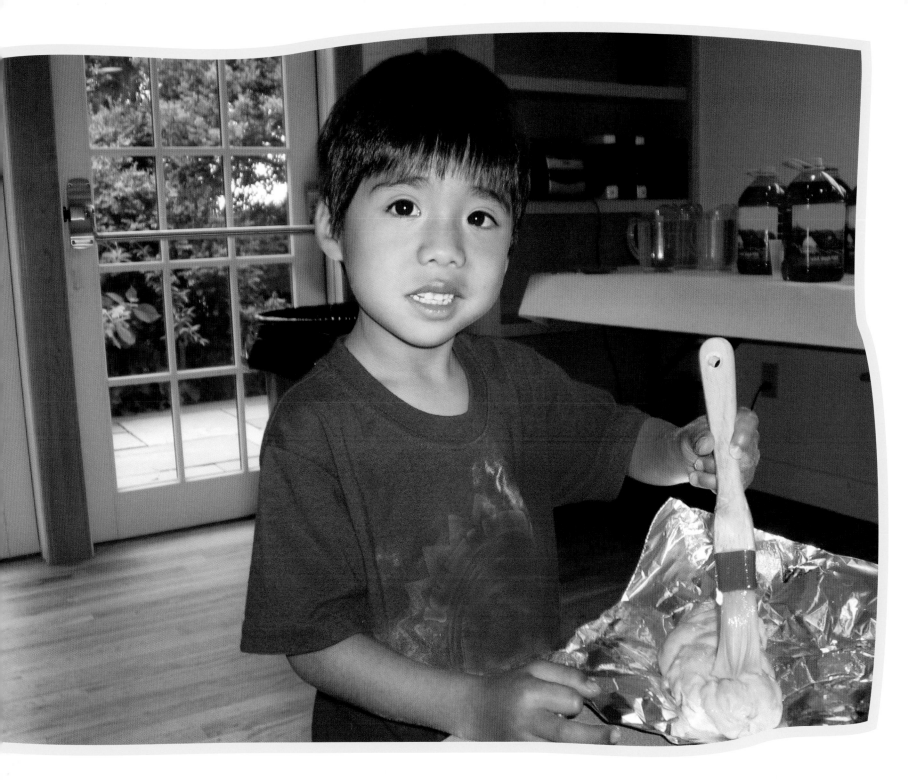

How do I know if I'm Jewish enough?

Will God dislike me if I don't do all this stuff?

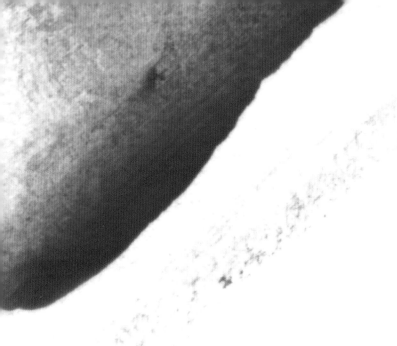

Just be the best person
       you can possibly be,
If you're **thoughtful**,
       nice,
       and
       honest
       you are living Jewishly.

When you do a good deed
that's being Jewish too,
And one thing you can count on
is that God **ALWAYS** loves you.

But I'm only a kid, what can I do?

Can good deeds be done
by children too?

You can visit a grandparent,
　　　pick your toys up from the floor,
When mom or dad asks for quiet,
　　　　　don't say any more.

Try to bring a smile
              to someone who is sad—
Doing any of these things
              will surely make God glad.

And when you're older
   you can do even more as a Jew,
Like visit Israel,
   and be bar or bat mitzvah too.

But now you're already
old enough to see
That everyday
you can live your life
Jewishly.

Now I understand what it means to be a Jew,

It's **NOT** how you look or what others think of you.

Being Jewish is about my deeds, thoughts, and heart,

So now I know I'm off to a very good start!

Put your photo here!